Global Budgets versus Competitive Cost-Control Strategies

Global Budgets versus Competitive Cost-Control Strategies

Patricia M. Danzon

The AEI Press

Publisher for the American Enterprise Institute

WASHINGTON, D.C.

1994

To order call toll free 1-800-462-6420 or 1-717-794-3800. For all other inquiries please contact the AEI Press, 1150 Seventeenth Street, N.W., Washington, D.C. 20036 or call 1-800-862-5801.

ISBN 0-8447-7023-X

THE AEI PRESS
Publisher for the American Enterprise Institute
1150 17th Street, N.W., Washington, D.C. 20036

ISBN 978-0-8447-7023-9

Contents

President Clinton's Health Security Act proposes to extend health insurance coverage to 40 million uninsured Americans and to increase the depth of coverage for the majority of those who already have private or public insurance. At the same time, the act promises to reduce total health spending below status quo projected levels. All this is to be done without diminishing—indeed, while improving—the quality of health care. Economic theory, empirical evidence, and common sense all indicate that expanding health insurance tends to increase health care spending. An insured patient faces a lower point-of-purchase price for medical care and therefore tends to make more frequent visits to the doctor and more willingly accepts recommendations for additional care. This positive relationship between insurance and utilization has been demonstrated in expansions of Medicare and Medicaid and was demonstrated scientifically in the RAND health insurance experiment.[1] In health care reform, increasing health care utilization by the currently uninsured is presumably one goal of expanding coverage. Thus, the mechanisms whereby the plan proposes to achieve simultaneously a massive expansion of coverage and a reduction in health care spending, contrary to all prior experience, deserve careful scrutiny. These mechanisms are key to evaluating the claims that the quality of care will improve, not decline, and that the federal deficit will decrease, not increase.

The Clinton administration's approach to health care reform was built initially on competitive strategies embodied in managed-competition proposals. These strategies rely on removing obstacles to the efficient functioning of health insurance markets. But once distortions are removed, the competitive approach depends on informed consumer choices in competitive markets to control costs at appropriate levels. By contrast, the Health Security Act dilutes competitive cost-containment strategies to the point where they are likely to be ineffectual. Since the act also specifies predetermined goals for health care spending that are optimistic (or unrealistic) given the expansion of coverage, the weak competitive pressures are almost certain to fail.

The act therefore superimposes on the managed-competition model a structure of global limits on private and public sector spending. The global budgets are presented as a backstop, to be implemented only if competitive pressures fail to contain costs within the president's specified targets. But given the unrealistic spending targets and the emasculation of competitive forces, these regulatory constraints will almost certainly prove essential to meeting the spending targets. This experience will appear to validate the arguments that competitive private insurance markets cannot deliver cost-effective medical care within reasonable costs and hence will feed into the arguments in favor of reinforced regulatory controls and perhaps ultimately a single-payer approach.

If these global spending limits are not enforced—and perhaps even if they are—government spending and hence the federal deficit could exceed the president's projections by billions of dollars. Even if the spending targets are enforced, the federal deficit could exceed projections if tax revenues fall short of forecast levels. But if these global spending limits are enforced, they will become the fundamental force that molds the evolution of our health insurance and health care delivery systems, including the quantity, quality, and availability of medical care and the development of new medical technologies.

Three key design features of the plan lead inevitably to the unpleasant choice between massive regulation and expanding federal deficits: (1) an extremely comprehensive guaranteed benefit package (GBP), (2) the promise to reduce health care spending, and (3) the political unwillingness to raise new taxes. In particular, in establishing universal coverage, the plan adopts a definition of covered medical services and a degree of financial protection that are more comprehensive than what the great majority of Americans currently purchase voluntarily, either directly or indirectly through their employers, even with the tax preference that subsidizes employer contributions and hence distorts the perceived cost of insurance below its true cost. Possible reasons for this choice of a Cadillac guaranteed benefit package include the desire to avoid the politically difficult issue of whether the guaranteed minimum level of coverage should also be the maximum; pressure from provider groups, which understand the business implications of being in rather than out of the benefit package; blind faith in the ability to cut costs without sacrificing quality; and strategic positioning, forcing anyone who proposes a more modest plan into the politically uncomfortable position of taking something away.

More coverage is better if it is free. But, in reality, someone has to pay. The polls apparently suggest that middle- and upper-income taxpayers are unwilling to pay significantly higher taxes to subsidize coverage for those who have no coverage or less comprehensive coverage. Therefore, those who will "receive" an increase in their coverage will largely be forced to pay for it themselves. This may be hidden through the mandate that employers contribute 80 percent of the cost for their employees and dependents. But, ultimately, this cost must be shifted to workers through lower wages or reduction in other benefits, if jobs are to remain.

This massive expansion of coverage is somehow to be reconciled with a reduction in total spending below status quo projected levels. The numbers can be made to add up only if the government controls the numbers and forces health spending down to the target level. But regulatory controls on spending, at most, control accounting costs. The real social costs of this strategy will be determined by the hidden costs. Some consumers will be forced to spend more on health insurance and hence will have to cut back on other, preferred consumption activities—including education, nutrition, and housing—that might have contributed more to improving their health. Others will be denied access to the quality of care that they would have been willing to pay for. Quality is multidimensional: obvious dimensions that will suffer under tight budget constraints include increased patient-time costs and inconvenience, loss of well-being and productivity due to limited access to care, and less access to innovative technologies. Arguments about loss in quality are often dismissed as the self-serving protests of providers and insurers. But while the immediate impact may be on providers' wallets, in the long run consumers—who are the intended beneficiaries of health care reform—will be the greatest losers.

Overview of the Competitive Approach to Health Care Reform

The competitive approach to health care reform recognizes that some government role is essential for universal coverage that is available to and affordable by all citizens. The essential functions of government are three: (1) to require everyone to obtain coverage, either through their employer, other groups, or individually; (2) to provide subsidies to ensure that the mandatory coverage is affordable for low-income and high-risk individuals; and (3) to implement the minimum set of insurance market regulations necessary to ensure that insurance is available to everyone. These minimum regulations include a guarantee the policies be renewable at class rates for a limited period (say, three years) without exclusions or restrictions for preexisting conditions. Thus, should a person contract a high-cost medical condition, the policy could not be canceled or restricted and could not be surcharged for a limited period. Community rating within classes, mandatory open enrollment, and a reinsurance facility may be useful to ensure access and affordability for high risks, depending on whether they receive additional subsidies directly.[2] In addition, provision of information to consumers about the plans available in the market could be useful. This could include coverage, premiums, and cost-control strategies. Outcomes and other quality indicators could be added when information systems are available to make this reliable and cost-justified.

The competitive approach to health care defines the appropriate or efficient level of spending as that chosen voluntarily by reasonably well-informed consumers when they face the full social cost of their choices. Thus, given a fixed set of subsidies that are designed to achieve equity goals and to make the required coverage affordable for everyone, consumers are free to purchase more comprehensive coverage with their own aftertax income and without additional subsidies. The current tax exclusion, whereby employer contributions are tax-exempt income to employees, distorts consumer choices because it is open-ended: the subsidy increases as more comprehensive coverage is purchased. Moreover, it is inequitable since the value of the subsidy increases with the employee's tax bracket. Because the tax exemption applies to federal and state income and payroll taxes, it is equivalent to a subsidy of more than 30 percent on average, up to at least 50 percent for those in high tax brackets. It is estimated to result in tax expenditures (lost potential tax revenues) of more than $60 billion.

Pure competitive strategies propose to eliminate the tax exclusion entirely and make employer contributions taxable income just like cash wages (or life insurance contributions beyond a threshold). The tax exclusion would be replaced with a system of refundable tax credits or subsidies targeted at low-income families and others for whom the required coverage would otherwise be unaffordable. A more limited approach would permit some tax-exempt contribution but would cap it at some fixed amount, above which all additional payments for health insurance or medical care would come from aftertax dollars, whether made by the employer or the employee, including cafeteria plans. This strategy would preserve the right marginal incentives since the cost of any additional coverage would be paid fully with aftertax dollars. The inequity of paying higher subsidies to higher-income taxpayers, however, would remain.

Once consumers face the full social cost if they choose to spend more on health insurance, there is no reason for the government to control these choices. The government has no superior insight into the appropriate level of spending of health care, and any limit other than one derived from consumer choices is as arbitrary when applied to health care as it would be for automobiles or videocassette recorders. Such arbitrary limits reduce consumer well-being since, by definition, they force consumers from their preferred consumption patterns.

If consumers are informed and face the full cost of their choices, there is no reason why competition in health insurance markets should not hold health insurance premiums and prices for medical services to appropriate levels. There is ample evidence that competing health insurance plans are aggressive and innovative in designing strategies to control insurance-induced excess spending (moral hazard.) These strategies include copayment structures, provider incentives such as capitation and prepayment, restrictions on choice, and utilization review. Although consumers may resent these restrictions if confronted with them when sick, consumers' actual choices indicate that most prefer to put up with some controls rather than pay the much higher premiums that would result from free care and unlimited choice. Thus, totally unmanaged, traditional fee-for-service plans have been losing market share to managed indemnity plans and point-of-service HMO plans. Managed indemnity leaves an unrestricted choice of provider but includes copayments and utilization review. Point-of-service HMOs have lower copayments if the patient stays within the limited network of providers, accepting gatekeeper management of all referrals for specialist care, but the patient can choose to seek care from a nonnetwork provider for a higher copayment.

In competitive markets, patients can choose the form and degree of control that they prefer. Insurers, in turn, compete by trying to design plans that provide a mixture of choice, quality, out-of-pocket cost, and premium cost that most appeals to consumers. Providers compete by their choice of prices, quality, and convenience. Although this view of the working of competitive markets for health care and insurance may seem inconsistent with some stories of policy cancellations, sharp price increases, and the like, in fact it fairly characterizes the broad trends for large-group health insurance and health care markets over the past decade, particularly where employers have taken an active role, together with employees, in managing their health care costs. The system is not perfect, but no system will be perfect. Some problems stem from government policies, including state-level benefit mandates and restrictions on competition, in addition to the tax exclusion already discussed. The goal of competitive approaches to insurance market reform is to remove these obstacles to a well-functioning market and to adopt the minimum set of regulations necessary to extend the conditions now available for large groups to smaller groups and individuals.

In contrast to this, the Health Security Act includes a global limit on total private spending on services in the guaranteed benefit

5

package; premium regulation for health plans; price regulation for medical services billed on a fee-for-service basis; mandatory health alliances that are the exclusive source of coverage and control which health plans can be offered; a regulated copayment structure; and restrictions on HMOs. In promoting the plan, the administration has emphasized that it preserves the patient's choice of physician. This is done by mandating that HMOs offer a point-of-service option and that at least one fee-for-service plan be offered, run by the alliance or by Medicare if no private plan is willing to stay in business. This promise of choice of physician does not extend to choice of plan outside the alliance system. The promise may be empty if approved plans are so constrained that providers have little flexibility in their choice of practice style.

Defining the Guaranteed Benefit Package

The president has stated that his sole, nonnegotiable demand is to assure universal health insurance coverage. This still begs three fundamental questions: (1) Should the guaranteed universal minimum coverage also be a universal maximum, or can individuals supplement this basic level without restriction? (2) What medical services are included in the guaranteed coverage? (3) What are the limits on financial exposure (maximum out-of-pocket cost) for the covered services? Additional (presumably, more negotiable) issues that must also be addressed include who will pay for the system and whether the insurance will be delivered through a single public monopoly or through private insurance markets. If the latter, how will it be regulated?

The answer to the first question—whether the goal is to assure a basic level for everyone but with freedom to supplement or a uniform, one-size-fits-all system—tends to dictate the remaining choices. Indeed, if the president's nonnegotiable demand is interpreted to mean universal coverage as defined in his plan, then much of the remaining regulatory structure of mandatory alliances and global budgets becomes inevitable.

Consider first the design of the guaranteed benefit package under the first choice, that everyone should have a basic level of coverage, with appropriate subsidies to assure affordability, but that everyone should be free to supplement any dimension of that coverage with their own aftertax income. If the only reason for mandating coverage is that some people are myopic, buy too little insurance, and end up forgoing necessary care when sick, then the mandatory benefit package should be the lowest common denominator; that is, it should include only those services that would be preferred by those with the lowest demand for medical care when they make informed, rational choices. Those who prefer more comprehensive coverage would be free to purchase it. With this approach, people would have the health insurance that they would choose if well-informed and would not be forced to spend more on health care than they would voluntarily choose. The poor, however, would probably buy minimal coverage and consequently receive minimal care.

More realistically, the prevalence of public hospitals and charity care indicates that our society views medical care as a merit good; that is, we as a society are unwilling to deny basic medical services to those who cannot pay for themselves. This merit-good rationale for universal coverage implies that, in defining the guaranteed benefit package, the relevant question is, What medical services would taxpayers be willing to subsidize for others who lack the means to pay for themselves? A full answer to this question requires specifying dimensions of quality as well as quantity of medical services, for example, freedom of choice of provider, geographic access, and waiting times for covered services.

This approach does not automatically yield a perfect blueprint for the guaranteed benefit package. Taxpayer preferences are hard to measure, heterogeneous, and depend on how the burden of paying is allocated. Nevertheless, this approach does provide a clear conceptual framework to address the problem, even if implementation is imperfect. To illustrate, assume that subsidies to the poor are to be financed from general revenues, primarily income taxes. Core services should then be defined to include all those that taxpayers would be willing to pay for or partially to subsidize for the poor, given the structure of general revenue financing. The availability of free or subsidized care for the needy, however, creates incentives for others to free ride and avoid payment for their own insurance in the knowledge that care will not be denied if needed. To preempt such free riding and the associated cost shifting, everyone must be required to obtain at least the guaranteed level of insurance protection, including those whose income exceeds the level that qualifies for a subsidy.

This approach to defining core services is fundamentally a benefit-cost approach, based on willingness to pay. For those people who will receive some subsidy, the benefit side of the calculus also includes the willingness of other taxpayers to subsidize their care. Since, for most people, the willingness to pay for others is likely to be no greater than the preferred level of services and willingness to pay for oneself, the guaranteed benefit package can be defined simply by reference to what taxpayers are prepared to finance for the poor. Since this is likely to be no greater than most people would choose for themselves, no consumers are forced to buy more than they want, and all are free to buy as much as they want. This supplementation can take the form of purchasing higher "quality" coverage for basic services, for example, coverage with more choice of physician, more prompt access to services, and lower patient-time costs. This is the approach of the British National Health Service, which places no constraints on the purchase of private insurance. Such coverage is purchased by an increasing percentage of the population. Private policies typically cover services in private hospitals and private sector physician fees, enabling policyholders to avoid the long waits for NHS services. This is not unconstrained freedom to supplement, however, because the individual who buys private insurance gets no rebate for the costs avoided by the NHS as a result of the use of private sector services.

Defining the guaranteed benefit package in principle requires ranking services in order of net benefit (benefit minus cost), where benefit is the willingness of society to pay. All services with positive net benefit should be included. In practice, it might be easier to determine the government budget for health care subsidies, based on taxpayer willingness to pay, and then include services starting with those who have highest expected net benefit. The list of covered services or the budget can be adjusted as experience accrues on costs relative to allocated funds. Because of the huge information requirements, it is surely best to start with a general definition of core services, possibly augmented by a negative list of services that are not covered. The more generally the core is defined, the greater the freedom for patients and medical providers to choose among alternative therapies to meet treatment goals and the greater the flexibility in adjusting to technological change.

Defining core coverage also requires specifying a maximum out-of-pocket cost, or stop-loss, for the services included in the guaranteed benefit package. Efficiency and equity indicate that this stop-loss should vary inversely with income. Significant copayments deter the poorest from seeking care, whereas a higher-income family can afford to make greater copayments, up to a much higher maximum. Permitting middle- and upper-income families to purchase only "catastrophic" financial protection enables them to take advantage of the cost-reducing effects of high copayments. This also benefits others, since the presence of some price-conscious consumers in medical care markets makes physicians more cost-conscious in their practice patterns and hence controls costs for others.

The only role for a global budget in this approach is a limit on government health spending, including any tax expenditures. This is essential to sound allocation of government funds between medical care and other uses. It is also necessary to ensure that consumers face the full marginal cost if they purchase additional coverage. Open-ended subsidies, as exist under the current unlimited tax-exclusion of employer contributions, leave government spending open-ended, distort consumer choices, and contribute to inappropriately high spending levels. An arbitrary limit on private spending on health care with aftertax dollars, however, is unnecessary and counterproductive. The level of health care spending by consumers who make informed choices in competitive markets, given the fixed set of subsidies as determined above, is the appropriate level of spending. Whereas limits on government spending are essential to efficient resource allocation to health care, arbitrary limits on private spending reduce social welfare.

The alternative view of universal coverage is that the mandatory minimum level of coverage should also be a mandatory maximum; that is, supplementary coverage outside the guaranteed benefit package should not be permitted. A modification of this view is that supplementary coverage should be banned for the services that are in the guaranteed package but permitted for noncovered services or amenities. Supplementary coverage, for example, could be purchased for cosmetic surgery or for a private room, if these are excluded from the basic package. Canada adopted this approach: private insurance is permitted only for services or amenities not covered by Canadian Medicare. Further, Canadian physicians who treat private patients cannot also bill for publicly financed patients.

This second view is implicitly adopted by the Health Security Act, which bans the sale of insurance outside the mandatory alliances for services included in the guaranteed benefit package. Supplementary insurance is permitted only for noncovered services or to cover copayments on covered services under the high copayment option. Because the list of covered services is extremely comprehensive, this restriction on supplementation is not as irrelevant as it may appear. This restriction effectively denies consumers the freedom to buy insurance that covers a higher "quality" of care for any and all services in the GBP. Thus the mandatory alliance system and ban on supplementary insurance for covered services effectively constrain everyone to the quality of care available under alliance-sponsored plans. The only exception is the cash purchase of covered services outside the alliance. Only those rich enough to pay cash can opt out, whereas the U.K. experience indicates that a significant number of middle-income people who lack the resources to pay cash would nevertheless be willing to pay for an insurance policy that assures them prompt access to costly surgical procedures by a physician of their choice.

Making the alliances the sole source of insurance for covered services would not matter if the alliances operated without global spending limits and were simply neutral brokers and conveyors of information, as in the original managed-competition proposals. But a ban on insurance outside the alliances is a real constraint when the alliances must enforce global spending limits and are authorized to disqualify plans that do not comply with their allocated premium targets. The tighter the global spending limits, the lower will be the quality of care that qualified plans can afford to offer and the greater the utility loss for consumers who would have been willing to pay for a different style of care or those who might have preferred higher quality on certain services but with higher copayments or no coverage of more marginally necessary services.

If the GBP is to be a ceiling as well as a floor for the quality and quantity of services, then the relevant design question is, What coverage would the average consumer be willing to purchase, after taking into account any taxes payable to subsidize the same level of coverage for others? (This average preference could be measured several different ways, for example, as a simple median preference or as a weighted average, with weights reflecting the intensity of preference for or against more comprehensive coverage.) Clearly, it is individuals who ultimately will pay, even if this is hidden initially through an employer mandate or by deficit financing. Preserving the fiction that the employer or the government pays permits politicians to promise more for less in the short run, but it is likely to lead to a different health care system than would emerge if the choices were posed explicitly.

The president's plan, characterized as comparable to at least the median of plans offered by the Fortune 500 companies, is more comprehensive than the average person appears willing to pay for voluntarily, even with the current tax subsidy, which, on average, reduces the cost of coverage by at least one-third. Thus, it is a fortiori more generous than most people would be willing to pay for if faced with the full cost. Because the tax exclusion is retained, insurance will remain significantly subsidized to middle- and upper-income consumers even under the reformed system. (Employer contributions to supplementary insurance will be taxable after 2004. Tax-sheltering employee contributions through cafeteria plans will be disallowed.) The politically acceptable GBP will therefore be more generous than if the tax subsidy were eliminated and everyone faced the real price of insurance.

The maximum permissible copayment levels—$1,500 for an individual, $3,000 for a family—are also lower than many middle- and upper-income families would probably prefer, given the potential premium savings from a policy with higher copayment. In the RAND health insurance experiment, total expenditures were 46 percent lower under a catastrophic plan (with 95 percent copayment up to a stop-loss of 10 percent of income), compared to totally free care. With a few specific exceptions, there was no evidence that this lower expenditure adversely affected patients' health, and those exceptions could easily be avoided by a well-designed catastrophic plan that would afford more complete protection for lower-income families. This evidence clearly refutes the common assertion that copayments lead consumers to forgo necessary care, leading to higher costs later. By regulating copayments, the Health Security Act imposes unnecessary costs for those who prefer to control their own medical spending, purchasing insurance only for catastrophic costs. It makes consumers less price-sensitive and reduces competitive pressures in medical markets and thereby exacerbates the case for regulatory controls.

The basic choice—between a guaranteed floor for all, with freedom to supplement, or a uniform system for all—is a philosophical and political choice that different societies have answered differently. Mandating a single, uniform coverage necessarily requires some to pay for more comprehensive coverage than they prefer and constrains others to less than they prefer. These discrepancies impose real social costs on consumers in terms of forgoing other consumption or forgoing medical care. These costs are avoided if the GBP is a base, corresponding to the level that we are willing to provide for everyone, with freedom to supplement for those who want more. Thus, mandating a uniform level of coverage can be optimal only if, on average or in aggregate, taxpayers consider that their personal utility loss from being forced to have too much or too little coverage is a price worth paying for a uniform or single-tier system. This acceptance seems to be assumed by the Health Security Act. But it warrants careful scrutiny since the design of a generous benefit package drives the demand for medical care and health expenditures. This, in turn, will confront Congress with the unpleasant political choice of regulating spending limits or adding to the federal deficit and the burden on future generations.

Mandatory Exclusive Alliances

Another rationale for banning insurance for covered services other than that offered through the mandatory alliances is to enforce the system of cross-subsidies implied by the mandatory community rating structure. Qualified health plans are required to charge a single rate for all enrollees, adjusted only by four family-size classes and two age groups (younger or older than sixty-five). Actuarially fair premiums could differ severalfold within each age group. Mandatory participation in these exclusive alliances is therefore essential to prevent opting out by lower risks. Given the mandatory risk pool, community rating effects massive cross-subsidies from low risks to high risks, without making these subsidies explicit.

Earlier managed-competition proposals denied any tax preference to insurance purchased outside the alliances but did not ban such insurance outright. The Health Security Act's outright ban on insurance of GBP services outside the alliances reflects the fact that, for many low risks, the implicit "tax" that they would pay through the community-rated premium would far exceed the value of their tax subsidy, which would be negligible for many young, healthy adults with low incomes. Thus, the carrot of tax subsidies would not induce participation by many low risks, and the stick of regulation becomes essential to prevent the risk pool from unraveling. If some low risks opted out, the contribution required by those remaining would increase, which would induce additional opting out and so on. Thus, making the alliances the exclusive source of mandatory coverage is an essential component of the plan, if comprehensive coverage is to be affordable to high risks without explicit subsidies.

High risks could be subsidized in other ways than mandatory community rating and exclusive alliances. These include direct subsidies to individuals or indirect subsidies channeled through a reinsurance facility. Several arguments favor these approaches over the hidden subsidies of community rating. First, direct subsidies can be targeted more effectively at the truly needy (not all high risks are poor, not all low risks are wealthy). Second, community rating exacerbates the incentives for insurers to attempt to skim the cream and therefore magnifies the difficulty for the alliances of making accurate risk-adjusting payments between plans. Third, political decisions about transfers are more likely to reflect taxpayers preferences if the taxes and subsidies are explicit. While such transparency may be good for taxpayers, however, it may be bad for politicians.

Financing

Mandating that everyone's coverage be raised to the level of the most generous plans currently purchased would benefit those who currently lack such coverage—if someone else paid for it. But that is not the case—not surprisingly, since polls indicate relatively low willingness to pay higher taxes to subsidize coverage for others. Under the Health Security Act, everyone is implicitly required to pay for coverage. This is hidden by the requirement that employers contribute 80 percent of the premium for employees and their dependents. But, in the long run, the employer contributions must be shifted to workers in the form of lower wage rates if job opportunities are to remain unaffected. A more accurate long-run view of the financing of the plan is that employees pay for 100 percent of the cost of their coverage, as is explicitly required of nonworkers. The Congressional Budget Office has recommended that the employer payments be treated as taxes. Logical consistency suggests the same categorization for the contributions made by individuals, since these are also mandatory. Calculations of winners and losers should assign the employer contribution to the employees who ultimately pay.

Explicit subsidies are provided only for those not covered through employment if their family income falls below 150 percent of the poverty line. Lewin-VHI estimates that the premium for a two-parent family in 1998 will be roughly $6,000, even with the budget caps. For a family with an income of $25,000, which is likely to exceed the 150 percent of poverty threshold for federal subsidy, the mandatory premium contribution will exceed 20 percent of that income. For employees with income up to $40,000, the employee 20 percent contribution to the premium is capped at 3.9 percent of income. If this cap is binding, however, their total contribution, assuming that they pay the employer's 80 percent indirectly through a wage offset, could again exceed 20 percent of income. This burden on low-wage workers may be mitigated if the subsidies payable to small firms with low average wages are also passed on. But this subsidy system is haphazard in targeting funds to those in need. Such subsidies are not available to low-income workers in larger firms; conversely, some subsidy dollars may be wasted because not all low-wage workers in small firms are from poor families. Thus, many low- and middle-income workers will indirectly be required to pay for coverage that is more comprehensive and therefore more costly than they would voluntarily choose.

Cost Control

It would be political suicide to propose a plan that explicitly mandates everyone to buy coverage as comprehensive as that currently selected by a minority of large firms with the tax subsidy. Yet the Health Security Act implicitly does this. Critical to making this strategy politically feasible are the employer mandate, to hide the incidence of the cost, and the global budgets, to hide the magnitude of the potential cost. Reconciling the potentially incompatible goals of increasing insurance coverage and reducing total health care spending is achieved by fiat of the National Health Board, which is empowered to specify both coverage and spending limits, requiring that plans somehow adapt the delivery of care to comply with these two requirements. Promised savings from managed care and administrative costs also are important in reconciling the numbers.

Competition. The plan claims to rely primarily on competition among qualified health plans to control premiums, with global spending limits and premium regulation to be available only if needed. But the plan emasculates the potential for competition to control costs. First, the open-ended tax exclusion of employer contributions remains largely intact, except that employer contributions to supplementary insurance are taxable after the year 2004 and the cafeteria plan loophole, whereby employee premium payments and copayments are tax-sheltered, is closed.

Second, a key design feature of competitive approaches is that tax-favored contributions by employers (or subsidies from the government) should be based on the least-expensive qualified plan. This forces the employee to pay the full incremental cost of selecting a more costly plan with aftertax dollars, thereby making employee choice more price sensitive, which, in turn, puts pressure on plans to control costs. By contrast, the Health Security Act requires employers to contribute at least 80 percent of the weighted average premium (WAP). The employee who selects a plan with a premium equal to the WAP pays at most the 20 percent with aftertax dollars. At least 80 percent of the difference between the least-costly plan and the WAP is tax-subsidized; the tax subsidy applies to the full differential if the employer contributes the full 100 percent of the WAP. Only if an employee opts for a plan with a premium above the WAP does that person pay the full incremental cost with aftertax dollars.

Thus, for plans with premiums below the WAP, unsubsidized consumer price-consciousness applies to at most 20 percent of the premium. A true premium differential of $300 is perceived as only $200 for an employee in a 33 percent tax bracket (a plausible average, including federal and state income and payroll taxes), $150 or less for families in the highest tax brackets. If an employee can get $300 worth of additional coverage by paying only $150, incentives for choosing a plan with a below-average premium are undermined. In turn, the incentives for plans to charge premiums below the average are undermined. If everyone attempts to charge at least the average, the average moves up. Thus, retention of a tax subsidy that cannot be less than 80 percent of the WAP and is open-ended up to 100 percent of the WAP will tend to fuel inflation of average premiums. A similar effect applies to employees and other individuals who receive federal subsidies. If these subsidies are based on the WAP, all subsidized individuals have little incentive to choose a plan that costs less than the WAP, unless they receive a cash rebate for the difference. Even if such rebates were available and consumers make cost-conscious choices, in practice the hassle and paperwork involved in processing such claims might deter many from opting for low-cost plans.

Employer contributions to supplemental insurance are tax-exempt until the year 2004, and supplemental insurance premiums are exempt from the global spending limits. This structure creates incentives for employees who prefer more generous coverage to obtain it in the form of a supplementary insurance policy rather than as a more comprehensive basic policy for which tax subsidies apply only up to the WAP. Other restrictions on supplemental insurance, particularly the prohibition on covering services in the GBP, however, may preclude the use of supplementary insurance to satisfy demand for higher-quality coverage.

Since the forces fueling insurance demand remain but the ability of insurers to offer policies that satisfy this demand is restricted, excess demand for the higher-quality and higher-premium plans within the alliances is likely. But alliances are authorized to exclude plans costing more than 120 percent of the average premium and to limit enrollment in those above-average premium plans that remain. How the limited spaces will be rationed remains speculation. Waiting lists, random allocation, and political favoritism are all possibilities, all of which will result in inefficiency and frustration of consumers' ability to satisfy their true willingness to pay for medical care. The rich may buy their way around these constraints since cash payments for medical care are excluded from the global budget limits. Thus, the constraints fall most heavily on those middle-income consumers who would have been willing to pay for insurance that would assure them prompt access to nonemergency services and unrestricted freedom to choose their own specialist or hospital.

Administrative Costs. The promised savings in administrative cost seem implausible in view of the increased regulatory requirements on plans, their need to increase controls in order to comply with premium limits, and the massive new regulatory structure. Use of uniform billing forms may simplify paperwork, but such savings will be limited unless there is a real reduction in the range of plans or coverage options offered. To the extent that the range of coverage options does decrease—and significant reduction is indeed likely, given the numerous constraints—there may be a significant loss in consumer utility that must be offset against any savings in administrative cost to determine the social cost. Since plans already have strong competitive incentives to incur administrative expense only to the extent that this yields at least commensurate benefits to consumers, forced changes are likely to result in a net efficiency loss, if correctly measured.[3]

Offsetting any gains from uniform billing forms (which arguably may be negative), enforcement and compliance with the massive new regulatory system will entail increased costs, both for health plans and for the operation of the alliances. Health plans required to operate within premium constraints will incur higher information and data expense related to defining and enforcing cost-reducing protocols. To avoid such costs, they may resort to more arbitrary rationing, which would impose higher hidden costs on patients. Health plans will also incur costs of complying with the data demands of the alliances, including information on outcomes, resource inputs, and risk mixture.

In addition to these new overhead costs for health plans, the alliances will incur costs related to their many functions, including evaluating plans, determining which are qualified, and negotiating premiums so that the alliance as a whole complies with its global budget allocation; collecting and disseminating data on qualified plans; managing the enrollment process; collecting premiums from employers and employees and sorting out requirements for families with multiple workers and hence multiple employer contributions; means-testing individuals and administering income-related subsidies to individuals; assessing the risk mix of each plan and implementing risk-adjusting transfers; assessing penalties against plans that exceed their spending limits; and negotiating an areawide fee schedule, to be used for all medical services paid on a fee-for-service basis. (To be done accurately, the risk-related functions would require detailed information on the risk status of each enrollee; currently, medical underwriting is not applied to the majority of those with private health insurance, who are covered through medium and large firms.)

Managed Care. The increased use of managed care is projected to yield savings of $14.9 billion, or a 20 percent offset against the projected increase in utilization of $58.6 billion.[4] These savings are characterized as increased efficiency and elimination of waste, permitting delivery of a higher quality of care at lower cost. To expect significant managed-care savings without binding premium controls and to characterize the changes as efficiency enhancing, however, is optimistic. In the 1970s and 1980s, HMOs derived savings relative to unrestricted fee-for-service (hereafter, pure indemnity) plans by reducing hospital admissions and length of stay. Even at that time, copayments had been shown to reduce expenditures in indemnity plans to levels comparable to those in HMOs.[5]

Since then, many indemnity plans have adopted utilization review and other strategies that have eliminated the differential in inpatient days. Indemnity plans are also adopting managed outpatient drug benefit schemes, so this potential source of cost differential is eliminated. Not surprisingly, premium costs for indemnity plans are often below those of HMOs that offer a comparable range of services, although copayments for indemnity plans are higher. If savings from a reduction in inpatient days have largely been exhausted, it is hard to see where the large managed-care savings can come from other than from a real reduction in access to or quality of services. This could include more stringent gatekeeper screening, eliminating some specialist care or substituting generalists for specialists; more limited access to costly technologies, even if they have fewer side effects, lower patient-time costs, or greater patient convenience; and longer waits for access to services considered elective, including access to specialist consultations. While some of these controls may reduce cost without impairing quality, this is not always the case for all patients. The recent growth of point-of-service plans and the stagnant market share of staff-model HMOs indicate patients' preferences for less control, even with more copayment.

Once global budgets are implemented and enforced by premium regulation, that the "savings" from managed care will suffice to constrain costs within the budget limits becomes a self-fulfilling prophecy. This becomes a necessary condition for health plans to survive. Survival as a qualified plan requires that the guaranteed range of services be provided at a premium acceptable to the alliance. Survival as a commercial entity requires controlling providers and patients so that expenditures for covered services do not exceed the regulated premium. Alliance spending caps are projected to yield an additional $47.3 billion in savings.

The coverage dimensions available to plans to control costs are severely restricted. For fee-for-service plans, the binding constraints are a regulated fee schedule, a prohibition on balance billing by providers, and limits on patient copayments per unit of services and on total out-of-pocket costs that are relatively low, given the comprehensive range of services that must be offered. Fee-for-service plans are also restricted from excluding providers. These restrictions on plans to adjust copayments or to permit providers to balance bill severely limit the strategies whereby free-choice indemnity plans have traditionally controlled insurance-induced excess demand (moral hazard).

It is a mistake to view the higher copayments that indemnity plans have traditionally charged, or their acquiescence in balance billing, as exploitation of consumers. On the contrary, such plans survive and are selected by a significant fraction of consumers because these consumers prefer this strategy for controlling moral hazard rather than the more hidden controls used by managed-care plans. Managed-care plans have lower copayments, but they control utilization through provider incentives—such as capitation, monitoring, and protocols—that affect providers' incentives to make costly services available to patients. Patients who prefer to have more say in how their use will be controlled prefer indemnity plans that rely more on patient copayment and less on hidden provider incentive structures and hidden rationing. Both strategies can achieve comparable cost savings relative to unrestricted choice with no copayment, and there is no compelling theory or evidence that the provider-targeted strategies of managed care lead to better care for a given cost than the patient-targeted strategies used by indemnity plans, including copayment and utilization review. The growth in market share of point-of-service plans indicates that many consumers are willing to pay higher copayments in return for greater freedom of choice.

By requiring that all plans offer a menu of services more comprehensive than that currently selected by most consumers, with regulated copayments that are lower than those selected voluntarily by many patients for a more limited array of services, the Health Security Act will severely hamstring the ability of fee-for-service plans to compete and to survive under global budgets. At the same time, HMOs' flexibility in controlling their costs is also constrained by the requirement that they offer a point-of-service option. This is a severe limitation if the regulated copayment limits are defined to include payments made to out-of-network providers.

Given these constraints, the only coverage dimensions that a qualified health plan can control to bring costs within the regulated premium are quantity and quality of the mandated services. Thus, the dimensions that must suffer are access to costly services and quality. The experience of the British National Health Service, which similarly forces providers to operate within tight budgets, indicates that the quality dimensions that are likely to suffer will include fewer referrals to specialists and longer waits to see a specialist once a referral is obtained; fewer elective procedures and longer waits; generic and therapeutic substitution of drugs (older, cheaper alternatives despite the risk of lower efficacy and more side effects); and substitution of cheaper, but less powerful, diagnostic equipment (for example, X-rays or old-generation CAT scans rather than magnetic resonance imaging [MRI]).

The regulated fee schedule, which is mandatory for all plans within each alliance that reimburse on a fee-for-service basis, is likely to generate higher hidden costs in the form of patient-time costs. The evidence from countries such as Germany, Japan, and Canada that have adopted such fee schedules is that, as the fee per unit of service is reduced, physicians reduce the real services provided per billable unit. This means shorter visits and fewer services per visit; hence, more visits must be made to achieve the same medical care. Each visit to the medical care system entails fixed time costs for the patient in the form of travel time, waiting in the office, and start-up costs of resuming whatever activity was interrupted to make the visit. In countries that rely solely on fee schedules to control physician expenditures, these hidden patient-time costs could amount to a real social cost of 10–100 percent of the cost of the physicians' services.[6] These hidden costs borne by patients, as well as the loss in well-being and productivity that result from queues for nonemergency services, are real social costs. Because they are not reported in accounting statements, however, they are excluded from the global budgets set by the National Health Board and from the estimates of health care spending. Thus, global budgets, if enforced, will control spending to comply with targets. But the real social costs under this strategy are likely to be much higher.

Concluding Comments

The president has said that his single nonnegotiable demand is universal coverage. But if that is defined as coverage as comprehensive as proposed in the Health Security Act, then the other dimensions of the plan will tend to follow. Upper-income taxpayers show no enthusiasm for paying for such generous coverage for those at lower incomes, so everyone must be forced to pay for themselves, with the exception of the poorest. It is politically impractical to require that a family of four with annual income of $25,000 must themselves pay a premium of more than $6,000 for this comprehensive coverage. Even if this were politically feasible, it would imply an increase in total health care spending that the president has promised to reduce. Therefore premiums must be limited, and the incidence of the cost must be hidden. This leads inevitably to global budgets and employer mandates.

If a private insurance market is retained, it is impractical to enforce global budgets except in the form of premium caps implemented at a local level. The alternative that has been used in other countries—global spending limits on the major components of health care services, for example, budgets for hospitals, physician services, drugs—are always leaky because some services are excluded. Such service-specific limits are also blatantly inefficient and encourage each provider group to shift costs to someone else's budget while discouraging efficient substitution of services. To cite a recent example, the physician drug budgets introduced in Germany in 1993 for primary care physicians have allegedly led to a 30 percent reduction in drug spending by general practitioners but have increased referrals to specialists and hospitalizations. Moreover, such service-specific limits violate the basic principle of managed care, which seeks to achieve an efficient integration of all modes of medical care.

If global spending limits are to be enforced locally and through insurance premium caps—which seems the most practical alternative given the current structure of the U.S. insurance market— then implementation requires some mechanism such as mandatory alliances to determine premium levels for each plan and to enforce compliance. The federal National Health Board could simply mandate that all insurance plans cut premiums by, say, 10 percent, but the arbitrariness of the limits would be more evident. Mandatory and exclusive alliances are also necessary if high risks are to be subsidized through the hidden taxes of community rating rather than through more direct and open subsidies, such as subsidies to reinsurance pools.

Universal coverage and reasonable cost control can be achieved through competitive strategies that will leave most people better off. This means designing a benefit package based on two simple principles. First, insurance is intended to protect against major, unpredictable expense, not routine costs. Second, more inquiry is needed into what citizens are willing to pay for health insurance, relative to other goods and services, for themselves and for others. Mandating that everyone pay for more insurance than they really want necessarily leads to regulatory controls and hidden costs that could more than offset the benefits of achieving universal coverage.

Notes

1. Willard G. Manning, Jr., et al., "Health Insurance and the Demand for Medical Care: Evidence from a Randomized Experiment," *American Economic Review*, June 1987, pp. 251–77.

2. If subsidies to individuals are adjusted on the basis of risk status to reflect the higher expected premium costs faced by those with costly medical conditions, there is less need for regulations that force transfers to high risks through insurance markets. These alternatives are described in Mark V. Pauly, Patricia Danzon, Paul J. Feldstein, and John Hoff, *Responsible National Health Insurance* (Washington, D.C.: AEI Press, 1992).

3. The productive role of spending on administrative functions is discussed in Patricia Danzon, "The Hidden Costs of Budget-constrained Health Insurance Systems," in Robert B. Helms, ed., *American Health Policy: Critical Issues for Reform* (Washington, D.C.: AEI Press, 1993), pp. 256-92.

4. These figures are from Lewin-VHI projections for 1998.

5. Manning et al., "Health Insurance and the Demand for Medical Care."

6. Danzon, "Hidden Costs."

About the Author

PATRICIA M. DANZON is the Celia Moh Professor of Health Care Systems and Insurance at the Wharton School of the University of Pennsylvania. She held positions at the University of Chicago, Duke University, and the RAND Corporation. Ms. Danzon has been widely published in the fields of health care, insurance, and liability systems. The author was recently elected to the Institute of Medicine of the National Academy of Sciences. She has served as a consultant on international health care issues to the World Bank, the New Zealand government, the Asian Development Bank, and the U.S. Agency for International Development.

Ms. Danzon is an adjunct scholar of the American Enterprise Institute.

AEI Studies in Health Policy

Special Studies in Health Reform

CLINTON'S SPECIALIST QUOTA: SHAKY PREMISES, QUESTIONABLE
CONSEQUENCES
David Dranove and William White

ECONOMIC EFFECTS OF HEALTH REFORM
C. Eugene Steuerle

THE EMPLOYMENT AND DISTRIBUTIONAL EFFECTS OF MANDATED BENEFITS
June E. O'Neill and Dave M. O'Neill

GLOBAL BUDGETS VERSUS COMPETITIVE COST-CONTROL STRATEGIES
Patricia M. Danzon

HEALTH REFORM AND PHARMACEUTICAL INNOVATION
Henry Grabowski

IS COMMUNITY RATING ESSENTIAL TO MANAGED COMPETITION?
Mark A. Hall

THE PUBLIC'S MANDATE ON HEALTH REFORM
Karyln H. Bowman

UNHEALTHY ALLIANCES: BUREAUCRATS, INTEREST GROUPS, AND
POLITICIANS IN HEALTH REFORM
Henry N. Butler

Other AEI Books on Health Policy

HEALTH POLICY REFORM: COMPETITION AND CONTROLS
Edited by Robert B. Helms

AMERICAN HEALTH POLICY: CRITICAL ISSUES FOR REFORM
Edited by Robert B. Helms

HEALTH CARE POLICY AND POLITICS: LESSONS FROM FOUR COUNTRIES
Edited by Robert B. Helms

RESPONSIBLE NATIONAL HEALTH INSURANCE
Mark V. Pauly, Patricia Danzon, Paul J. Feldstein, and John Hoff

REGULATING DOCTORS' FEES: COMPETITION, BENEFITS,
AND CONTROLS UNDER MEDICARE
Edited by H. E. Frech III

www.ingramcontent.com/pod-product-compliance
Lightning Source LLC
Jackson TN
JSHW011944131224
75386JS00041B/1563